table of contents

Ann Weimer Baumgardner
pretend you're normal

(but only when absolutely necessary)

going up?

I was never locked in a closet, but I did spend a lot of time playing in them. My first job was that of elevator attendant. I was four years old and worked the downstairs closet off the main hall of our house. It was one of those with double doors that slide. My mother was a smart woman who knew the lure of a small, well-lit space to a child. Together we pushed all the coats to one end, kicking the boots and stray mittens aside to make room. Mom set up a folding chair in the closet and gathered some picture books to keep me busy during off-peak hours. I fashioned an index card with floor numbers and buttons to tape to the closet wall. With a tug on the light-string, the elevator lit up, and we were ready for business.

As I turned the pages of my book, I kept an ear tuned—listening for my mother to step up, vacuum in hand, singing a single melodious "Ding!" This was my cue to slide open the door. "This vacuum," she'd say, "is awfully heavy. Would you mind taking me up to the second floor?" In my most professional voice I'd reply, "Certainly. Just step inside." I'd press the button on the index card that read "2," and we'd begin our ascent, staring blankly at the wall in that uncomfortable elevator silence until my "Ding!" signaled the opening of the doors. My mother would exit, thanking me again and again for helping her and promising to return soon. Mom knew just how long a kid could endure isolation and would stop by at regular intervals throughout the morning, requesting to be transported to new heights.

don't feed the animals!

We've all been to the zoo and know we're not supposed to feed the animals. But isn't the idea of it thrilling? Food tossed over the fence ravenously gobbled up in seconds by fierce lions? Pulling your fingers back just in time to feel the hot breath of a wild grizzly bear?

My dad had a ritual of feeding the tigers every Sunday night while he watched football and supervised the folding of the laundry. Hot dogs were the order of the day, cooked to perfection in our own living room over a roaring fire. While Dad cooked, my sister and I folded laundry behind the fireplace screen Dad had positioned in the corner. Once we'd sorted all the delicates, we were free to roam in our cage, unencumbered by loose laundry littering the floor, getting caught and snagged in our razor-sharp claws.

As we paced back and forth in our lair, growling and lunging at the smells and sights of food, Dad tore off pieces of hot dog and bun to throw over our wire cage. My sister and I enjoyed wrestling over the tiny morsels, anxiously waiting for the next bite. Dad felt lots of warm tiger breath on his hands but usually escaped being bitten.

While other dads just sat on the couch watching football, my dad was able to get all the laundry folded and experience the thrill of feeding hungry tigers. Not bad for a Sunday afternoon.

tucked in tight

Grandpa rode his stationary bike around the world. With his hand-made magazine rack fixed to the bike, he traveled through the pages of his *National Geographic*—bottle of H_2O by his side. He pedaled under the blazing sun of his shop light hanging from the ceiling joist overhead, guiding the way through foreign territory.

Grandma sat in her usual place in the swivel chair by the picture window with the encyclopedias she bought from a man she felt sorry for. She had read her way up through D before tiring of it and deciding that even though she hadn't finished them, she had learned quite enough.

My sister Jennifer and I announced our arrival with the bang of the screen door and a sing-song, "yoo hoo." We used to sleep over at Grandma and Grandpa's every Friday night. We'd walk over from our house, a street away, carrying our psychedelic 70's suitcases loaded with the essentials.

My grandparents were great babysitters. Before we could eat a cookie, we first had to eat something healthful like a wedge of cheese. But since Grandma considered cheese to be "binding," we then had to eat an orange. Fortunately her cookies were worth it.

The best fun was watching Grandma take out her teeth. From our bed we were able to see her reflection in the bathroom mirror. In the darkness of our room, a few moments later, we'd smell her freshly "Listerined" breath marching in before her. We'd each receive a loose-lipped kiss on the cheek and hear a wet and whistly, "Good night. Sleep tight. And don't let the bedbugs bite" spoken in German. (Shloffen-ze-vole. Lossen-dee-von-sin-neecht-vison).

It was always tough to sleep at Grandma and Grandpa's because the two of them had taken too many naps during the day and were up prowling the house all night checking on us and making sure they'd locked the doors. We would just get comfortable and start drifting off to sleep when we'd hear the floor boards squeaking, and Grandma would be tucking our legs back under the covers and pulling the blankets up to our chins. Once she'd go back to bed, Grandpa would get up and do the same thing.

One Friday night Jen was staying at a friend's house, and Grandma thought I'd get scared sleeping by myself, so she had me sleep between her and Grandpa in their double bed. I was used to Grandpa's sleeping noises because my ritual was to pretend to take a nap with him on the afternoons I visited. Once I got him to sleep, Grandma would let me come out and watch her "programs" with her. "Programs" is old-lady code for soap operas.

You've seen people who protect their sofas by shrink-wrapping them in protective plastic. Well, my grandma thought Grandpa drooled too much and wrapped his pillow in the same manner. The noise of his crackling pillow filled the room the way candies do in church when you try to quietly twist off the wrapper.

The worst part of the night, though, was the heat. As scared as I was to sleep alone, I would have gladly slept with monsters just to be comfortable. There I was, stuck between the two of them the whole night with the covers up to their chins, baking at high temperatures under wool blankets. In an attempt to expose some bare skin to cooler air, I pulled both legs to my chest and let my calves and feet peek out from the neck of the covers for a quick breath. After that awful night I learned to be brave and toughed it out with a night light across the hall from them. Besides, I knew I wasn't really alone because every ten minutes one or the other would be up to check the furnace, relock the doors and tuck me in.

thixth million dollar man

"Hey, Ann. Look at me. I'm (Th)teve Au(th)tin, Thixth Million Dollar Man."

Stevie Kwon, the four-year-old Korean boy bionically running and jumping down our driveway looked nothing like Lee Majors, who played the Six Million Dollar Man on TV. In fact Stevie, except for the echoing da-da-da-da-da-da-da noises he used for effect, had absolutely nothing in common with Lee Majors. Stevie's "lithp" was thicker than thick and far from the macho phenotype TV superheroes exude.

No, Stevie was the kind of boy who regularly cut his own hair, lovingly peed his name onto the sidewalk, rode his Big Wheel downhill backwards and once accidentally pooped in our front yard when time got away from him. Obviously, Stevie was unafraid of his mother, or mine for that matter, as my mom trumpeted the now-famous words on that fateful day, "Stevie, you take that home with you!"

Maybe this is how all bionic men get their start in life, but regardless, I, a pre-teenager, thought Stevie showed promise and decided to take him under my wing. I had a paper route business that could use a six million dollar man. Stevie rode side-saddle on the bar of my dad's bike while I pedaled. When we arrived at a house, Stevie would jump down, grab a paper and run it up to the door. Stevie delivered papers up one side of the street and down the other, while I made the reverberating sounds of Steve Austin's six million dollar legs. Singing theme music and making weird noises seemed a small price to pay for getting my papers delivered. I'm sure that by now, Stevie has lo(th)t the li(th)p, but I hope he hasn't lost his six million dollar magic that lit up the neighborhood.

to each her own flavor

It's a hot summer evening in the days before air conditioning. My family is sitting in the car while my dad goes up to the Dairy Queen window to place our order. He'll come back with one of those cardboard carrying cases they make to help cones stand up when two hands are not enough.

My mom twists around from the front seat, her eyebrows pinched together in a worried wrinkle, "Ann, are you sure you want chocolate? You tried that once before, and your dad had to finish your cone for you. You like vanilla. Remember? You don't have to like chocolate just because Jennifer does. Why don't you order a vanilla cone instead?"

My dad stands with all the other dads, dutifully lined up like children playing "Mother May I," each taking baby steps forward in line. As dad inches closer to the window, I get on my knees, lean my head out the window and yell a desperate, "VANILLA!" Dad's been expecting my call. This is our ritual. Vanilla. The last vestige of Ann. The only part that wasn't written over. A hiccup in the copycat process of a little sister who admired—to the extreme—her older sister.

As ice cream does, it melts. It drips. Over the years, that vestige of vanilla made its way into other areas of my life. I left science to become a writer; had one child instead of the usual two or three; and gave up Miss Clairol to go gray. Ann became Ann instead of a poor imitation of Jennifer.

trouble at grandma's

The phone rang. It was Allen Wandersleben, our good friend, who lived across the street from my grandparents. He wanted to talk to Dad right away. Dad's face showed worry as Allen expressed concern, saying, "George. I think something's wrong at your folks'. There's been no activity over there, and it's already eight-thirty in the morning." My grandparents were farm people who used to get up with the cows and by eight-thirty were nearly ready for lunch. Eight-thirty and the flag wasn't out yet; something was wrong.

We ran through the backyards and met Allen at the front of the house with keys. As Dad opened the door, we all scattered; Jen and I to the basement, Mom to the kitchen, and Dad and Allen down the hallway to the bedrooms. Grandma and Grandpa's bedroom door was shut, and my dad braced himself, not sure what to expect. Recently Grandpa had been diagnosed with Alzheimer's and was worried about being a burden to the family. Opening the door, Dad saw Grandma and Grandpa both still dressed in their night clothes lying peacefully in bed. Dad moved closer to investigate. As he leaned in to check their breathing, Grandma opened one eye and tittered, "You thought we were dead, didn't you?"

Dad and Allen broke into nervous laughter; Jen, Mom, and I joined them at the foot of the bed. "Grandma, why didn't you and Grandpa wake up this morning?"

"Well, you girls are always going on about how much fun it is to sleep in on Saturdays, so your Grandpa and I thought we'd try it. You were right; sleeping in is pretty exciting!"

weekends with nana

The widowers came calling on Nana once Pop-pop was gone. While they knocked on the front door, Nana snuck into her Jehovah's Witness hiding place half tucked behind the china cupboard where she couldn't be seen from the windows or the front door. "What would I want with another woman's old man?" she'd say when we encouraged her to visit with them.

Nana was happy living alone on the farm knitting slippers and tending her garden. She was famous for her love of flowers. Since the time she was a young bride, she'd been gathering different strains of daffodil bulbs, making her way each year a little farther down the road. By the time she hit her nineties there were nearly a mile of daffodils coming up each spring. Surreal, like something you'd see in the Wizard of Oz.

When I got my driver's license, I'd go out to her place to spend the weekend. The house felt so different in the dark. I saw things I didn't notice during daytime visits. My washcloth and towel were wrinkled and stiff from drying on the clothesline. There was no hot water except what you heated in the teakettle. Cows mooed at night, and the cicadas sang in swells.

I gathered my things to head up to bed. There was a door at the bottom of the stairs wearing layered years of white paint, its cut-glass door knob looking like a movie star's diamond ring. I liked the tap-tapping sound of my feet on the rubber mats lining the wooden stair steps as I made my way up. From the comfort of my mother's old feather bed, I looked for animal shapes in the watermark-stained wallpaper on the ceiling. Barnyard flies buzzed against the screens all night with a tenacity not found in suburban flies.

In the mornings I'd waken to Nana's high-pitched clearing of her throat and kitchen noises. She was a big believer in garlic and fried it with her eggs. On the rare occasion that we'd get a runny yolk, we liked to sop it up with some toast. I usually got sent to the basement to find some bread from the freezer. It wasn't really a basement. Real farmhouses don't have basements; they have cellars. Basements have laundry rooms, ping-pong tables, and workshops, while cellars have dirt floors, five-foot ceilings, strings of cobwebs, and are just plain scary.

Nana's cellar smelled like a carrot that had grown too big and had gotten all bitter and musty tasting. There were dark corners everywhere that the bulb on a wire couldn't reach, and every time I bumped my head on the light, it would start swinging—making all the shadows dance.

Nana had one of those coffin freezers with a lid that lifts up instead of a freezer that opens up neighborly… like you're coming to call. When I was in there head first, digging around looking for things, I always peeked over my shoulder to be sure the monsters weren't coming out of their hiding places to attack me.

With the Wonder Bread found, I'd grab it by its tail and with my other arm held high in the air, fish for the light string's sinuous thread. With a desperate tug I'd bolt up the stairs toward the warm noises of pans clanging in the kitchen. I was sixteen and too old to be afraid of monsters in a cellar, but you'd never know it as my heart raced up those crooked steps without me.

the great mid-west
furnace tournament

It's almost November, that awful time of year when it's one rainy day after another. The trees have lost their color, and the once pretty leaves now plaster wet driveways and fill up the gutters. The patio furniture is perched precariously in its winter home at the back of the garage. The porch swing, inviting on a summer day, now hangs up high, buried in the gray sky. During this gloomy time, when the holidays are a little too far around the comer, we mid-westerners help pass the time by taking part in the unofficial Annual Mid-West Furnace Tournament.

No one fully understands why we get this thrill out of NOT turning on our furnaces. Some might say suffering through frosty nights gives those of us who aren't good at sports a way to show our grit. But whatever the reason—pride, thriftiness or tradition—the furnace tournament seems to consume all of us. My ninety-five year old Nana, still living in her drafty old farm house, enjoys telling us about her bedside water glass freezing with a thin film of floating ice. Small talk after church and in elevators revolves around the sport. "Have you turned your furnace on yet?" "I heard we're supposed to get a hard frost tonight; this might be it for us."

My husband Erich and I are experienced players; a little frost won't scare us away. We had to make adjustments when our daughter Emily was first born, but now she's old enough that we simply swaddle her in blankets and footie pajamas and send her off to her wallpapered ice box where clowns look down on her with frozen smiles.

We don't mind sleeping in the cold, especially since we know some tricks for staying warm. Erich and I grew up in "tourney" families, so we're privy to some of the secrets passed down through the generations. In the old days, when people played this game out of necessity, my grandmother put hot potatoes in her pockets and slept with a soapstone fresh from the fire. My personal solutions to the cold aren't always so welcome. I still remember Erich's horror when he discovered that not only do I wear old sweatshirts and men's long underwear to bed (that front pocket is such a handy place to keep a tissue), but in extremely cold weather I sleep with my childhood baby blanket wrapped around my shoulders and neck to keep the breezes out. In the interest of romance and to help balance the shock of my appearance, I've taken to pre-warming my feet with the hair dryer before jumping into bed.

Regardless of our efforts, before long we lose our resolve and come to the realization that it's time. In quiet submission, we listen to the furnace rumble and belch its unmistakable first-use-of-the-season smell. We watch the hot-bitter air as it scatters dust bunnies into their dark corners. We console ourselves with thoughts of the upcoming holidays and congratulate each other on making it through another dismal November.

We try to keep in our minds the thoughts of spring time, when leaves will once again fill out the trees; gutters will flow with spring showers; patio furniture will make its way to the deck and the porch swing will be lowered to its normal height inviting neighbors to stop by for a chat to share their family's adventures in the Great Midwest Furnace Tournament.

Reprinted from Christian Science Monitor November 17, 2005

pretend you're normal

All my tennis shoes were green at the toe—the defining mark of a kid who mowed lawns. Our grass was mowed but never trimmed. Like a bad haircut, its bangs hung unevenly across the sidewalk and driveway. Dad bought the old kind of mower, the safe kind that won't cut off your toes. He'd pick them up at garage sales for a few dollars when all the dads were switching to the new ones. My friends had fathers who cut on the diagonal, were passionate about poisoning crabgrass and dandelions—fathers who edged. To my white-toed friends, mowing was a foreign country, a forbidden treat, and there we sat with three lawn mowers in the garage—a relay race just waiting to happen. My dad pulled them all out and lined them up in the front yard; kids formed rows waiting for their chance to race like a demon to victory. A yard that usually took forty-five minutes to mow was done in ten, albeit without the fancy golf-course-quality lines. It was cut... though it wasn't quite what you'd call normal. *Normal* has never been our family's forte.

Dad was always anxious to teach us somewhat dangerous

skills to show that he loved and trusted us. To him, a passionate carpenter, learning to safely catch a hammer when someone tosses it to you from upstairs is an important life skill that needs to be passed on to the children. "Stand to the side and stick your arm out. That way if you miss it, it will just hit the wall." Like a hammer hitting the wall isn't a problem. Sometimes he'd get the ladder out and help us climb around on the roof. As he coached me into releasing the death hug I had on the chimney, he'd say, "This is good for you; you don't want your first time on a roof to be when the house is burning."

My mom is better at "playing normal" than the rest of us. She wears pantyhose when it's appropriate, is a member of the Women's Club, and actually irons her clothes. From looking at her, you'd never guess that she had swings hanging in her basement and gave her children crutches and an old wheelchair for Christmas one year. Everyone wanted to play at the Weimers'; while waiting for our grass to grow, we practiced walking with crutches, played on the swings, rode unicycles, and took the wheelchair for a spin down Mitchells' hill.

We all knew how to be normal, when we had to. From nine to five Dad was investing millions of dollars as the Vice President of the trust department for our local bank, Mom was tutoring in the public schools, and my sister Jennifer and I were encouraged to study hard, go to church, and get involved in community service. We could pull it together for a job interview or a wedding ceremony, but when it didn't really matter, our family always preferred to do it the fun way.

A church breakfast could be done the usual way, or once when my dad was asked to plan it (and I do mean once), he made a lovely breakfast of green eggs and ham. Instead of the usual potted plant or candle as a centerpiece, he went with the less traditional "live bunnies in cages." Some guests were horrified, others delighted, as we choked down the eggs so we could be free to pet and play with the lovable table decorations.

In college I was asked to join several honoraries and, not knowing one from another, turned down Phi Beta Kappa because I was sick of the fees and paperwork. Little did I know that U.S. presidents list their membership in Phi Beta Kappa in their presidential résumés. On one of the honorary forms I filled out, I was asked what name I'd like printed on my certificate. They didn't ask what my name was, but rather what name I'd like on the certificate. I thought Annifer would be nice. My mother, well pressed and wearing panty hose, was totally shocked when the president of the college announced my name in royal fashion over the PA system as "Annifer Weimer." Following graduation protocol, I dutifully stepped forward to receive my honor and shake hands with the president. My dad beamed; I don't think I've ever seen him so proud. As we left the ceremony, he elbowed me in the side, giving me the fake reprimand we were often given before solemn functions, "Pretend you're normal!"

the bunny

I'm eating the legs off my daughter's forgotten chocolate Easter bunny. My husband and I keep sneaking away, nibbling it into oblivion. Huddled around the peanut butter jar, we take turns dipping bunny parts until there's nothing left of the helpless little creature but its plastic body bag. We bury the evidence in the bottom of the trash can, where it will hopefully remain undiscovered along with the thousands of nursery school art projects we can't possibly be expected to keep.

With the rabbit gone, we search the house for any remaining Easter candy and are disappointed to find only five jelly beans, all white, of course. In our house white jelly beans have as much chance of being eaten as a cow in India. It's not that we hold any reverence for them; it's just that we don't like them, and our generation won't eat what we don't like. My parents and grandparents, who lived through the Depression, will eat almost anything—the dry end of cheese, banana bruises and, of course, we've all seen them eat burned toast.

Although I can't bring myself to eat these things, I feel terribly guilty for throwing away good food. My solution to this dilemma is to wait until the food goes so bad there's no question what should be done with it. In a month or two, those jelly beans will be found by some lucky ants and then they, like the stuff in the vegetable drawer that's slowly melting into V-8, can be pitched into the trash with a clear conscience.

I'm just hoping that months from now, in one of those latent moments of clarity children are famous for, my daughter doesn't remember the chocolate Easter bunny we put to rest tonight. I know we'll be absolved if we can simply go undiscovered until the next holiday or birthday brings on another round of treats.

blaze of glory

I used to dress for bed like a bobsledder in the Winter Olympics; all that remained exposed to the night air were my eyes, nose and chin. But now that I've hit my forties, I'm experiencing a different side of life. Pajamas are a thing of the past. Not only do they make me too warm but they create extra drag, interfering with my ability to do unfettered flip turns in bed. I've tried slippery nightgowns and close-fitting tank tops, but nothing compares to the freedom of skinny dipping between the sheets. When traveling I start out with the best of intentions to stay jammied all night, but rarely do I wake up in them.

One weekend, my sister Jennifer and I brought our daughters to Mom and Dad's for a visit. We girls "camped" out in the basement with sleeping bags, blankets, and stuffed animals. In the middle of the night, I gingerly picked my way across the rubble, hoping not to step on a sleeping child as I made my way to the restroom. All was well until on my return my sister thoughtfully snapped on the light next to her bed, lighting a path back to my cot. There I stood, completely naked, blinking back the brilliant light, caught with my arms outstretched for balance, tiptoeing through a minefield of prostrate bodies both alive and stuffed. In the three seconds it took for my sister to gasp and flick off the light, my ten-year-old niece, Elaine, briefly lifted her head from her pillow.

Had she seen me? Was she just rolling over in her sleep? Perhaps the light was so bright Elaine didn't take it all in. Maybe I could hope for *blurry*. When I was safely in my cot, Jen and I choked on giggles the way we used to do in church. Our bodies shook; we held our stomachs. I made promises to pay for therapy while she chuckled over this rather imposing image of Aunt Ann forever burned in her daughter's brain.

The next morning I decided to test Elaine's memory. "Elaine. I don't know if you remember, but something really exciting happened last night; I think we were visited by an angel of the Lord. The angel appeared in a blaze of light with arms outstretched, shining in all her glory. And the funny thing was there wasn't a feather on her."

Elaine laughed saying, "That was no angel. That was YOU!"

When we get together at family gatherings, I sometimes ask Elaine if she's seen any angels lately, but fortunately for all of us, angel sightings are pretty rare.

the laundry

ome people take their dirty clothes to a Laundromat. Others take theirs to the cleaners. At our house we've found a better way to get our clothes folded; we invite Emily's friends over to play prison. We have a laundry room off the kitchen, where the prisoners receive folding instructions and take their meals. Every once in a while I growl and scowl like a good warden should, and I frisbee in slices of bread for the inmates. With the door open a crack, I inch a tin cup of water into their cell using the stick end of my broom.

Once they've folded a load or two, I let them know I've activated the motion detector and have turned off the lights. Crawling on their bellies with flashlights in hand, they attempt to flee from their imprisonment. "We-ooh, we-ooh," the alarm goes off. Children everywhere. I reach for the light. "ESCAPE, ESCAPE!"

"Can we play prison again, Mrs. Baumgardner?"

"I guess I can find a load of towels to throw in."

feeding the alligators

Over Christmas we spent a week with my sister and her daughters. Meg, the three-year-old, didn't want to use the bathroom at bedtime. Before we started drawing battle lines for the inevitable war, I decided to ask Meg why she would pass up a chance to feed the alligators. Of course Meg didn't know what I was talking about until I explained that the alligators were waiting for their bedtime snack of tinkle soup. She was thrilled to take part in such culinary delight and, as she finished up, remarked with considerable strain and a grimace, "I'm going to put a cherry on top." (A nice bonus we never expected).

We used "the alligators" for the rest of the week whenever we needed Meg to use the restroom before we headed out for a long car ride. Even my dad would grab a newspaper and announce to the family that he was going off to feed the alligators. Once, when I walked past the open bathroom door, I saw Meg leaning over the toilet, yelling down, "This one's from Meg," as she flushed. After a week of holiday festivities, you can bet the alligators in Westfield, New Jersey, were quite content.

the basement

Just below the surface of plush carpets, delicate china, and tidy rooms lies the basement, "the other world,"— a place belonging to children with its cement floors for roller skating, gray metal poles for shinnying, and exposed-joist ceilings where you can hang swings. A parallel universe where upstairs rules don't apply. Parents open the door only to announce mealtimes or to toss down a toy that spun beyond the borders.

Baby dolls littered our basement floor in various stages of nakedness. Gone are the days when beloved Buttercup and the others lived in the "upstairs world" where they were taken on family vacations, were fake-fed pieces of popcorn and were tucked under the covers and whisper-sung lullabies. Now they are basement dwellers with their clothes and hair smelling permanently of basement breath; cold, damp and musty. It's no wonder they became ill and fulfilled their new roles as patients in our pretend hospital ward. Temperatures were taken, shots were given, and homemade IV bags were hung from the basement clothesline.

My grandfather was always after us to dress our dolls. All that plastic flesh made him nervous. One poor nude soul he named Noodles, donating his sock as a makeshift dress to protect her modesty. Another unfortunate baby doll was Jiminy, a former "onesie" model my father purchased from the Jack and Joy's Children's Clothing Shop. In preparation for my impending birth into the family, Dad was sent out to find a lifelike baby doll to help my three-year-old sister better cope with my arrival. Dad somehow finagled the owners of Jack and Joy's into parting with their mannequin, who was "all boy," a rarity for that day and time. Jiminy's hard-formed-plastic body made him heavy and difficult to carry. No baby-doll clothes would fit him, so he wore a pinned diaper with a pink and white flowered flannel vest tied over his Buddha belly. Though completely bald and remarkably unattractive, Jiminy, like most real live boys, somehow managed to have the most gorgeous, thick, dark lashes glued just north of his frozen-open eyes. The mannequin mold he was poured from left him with a hole in his stomach the size of a soup can, making him our favorite critically-ill patient and frequent recipient of emergency "stomach pumpings" to extract toy cars, loose change and once a small rubber alligator. Jiminy's full name was Jiminy Cricket, so dubbed because of the live cricket discovered one day roaming the caverns of his plastic limbs.

After "Hospital" came "Office," where there were no starring roles for dolls. We rolled fake cigarettes to smoke at our desks with red markings on the end to resemble burning butts. Feeling very important in our make believe phone conversations, we shuffled papers and scrawled notes pretending to write in cursive, dotting nonexistent i's and crossing phantom t's. The dolls wouldn't come back into fashion until a middle-school slumber party, when they were dug from a box to serve as victims in our rendition of a murder mystery. Later that night they became props for three obsessed, schizophrenic clients in our game of "Psychiatrist," where therapy sessions were played out into wee hours of the morning.

Before long, carpeting arrived downstairs. Paneling was put up. We started accumulating a record collection for our new stereo. The basement became the place to practice being grown up in a new way, by kissing your boyfriend on the couch. We weren't quite ready to live fulltime in the world of plush carpets, fragile china and tidy rooms, but we were getting closer. Time passed. We went away to college. We married and had children of our own. The basement, still dressed in its 1970's orange shag carpeting and Peter Frampton posters, sat empty, waiting for our babies to become "basement age."

Pulling dress-up clothes and baby dolls from dusty hiding places, my sister and I finally introduced our daughters to the wonders of the basement. Looking at Buttercup with grown-up eyes, we saw her once-blond hair now matted into dreadlocks with parts of her scalp gone bald, showing evenly spaced blackheads where doll-hair implants used to be. Our girls were drawn to a box with feather boas, purses, and hats; they found a real majorette's outfit, complete with boots and baton. Meg found a costume jewelry box, announcing, as only Meg could, "Man.

Gram has bling!" Our children spent their uninterrupted hours in the basement, orchestrating dramas to be played out at the bottom of the stairs. We were summoned with home-made tickets and playbills grabbed by the hand and dragged to the basement steps, where we sat stadium style, playing our part as the adoring audience whistling and clapping for each player.

Now the children have grown. The basement sits quiet, used only as a pass-through to hang up laundry. As Mom and Dad empty closets and discard old playthings, we're forced to part with Noodles, Jiminy Cricket and Buttercup. The "make-out couch" is replaced with a hide-a-bed for overnight company. The basement has become regular and boring. The dehumidifier has removed all traces of basement breath, imaginary smoke from our cigarettes and the sound of applause. All of that wonderful pretending is erased except that it was good practice for life. If we never do anything truly fabulous in our real careers, we can die happy, knowing that together we've saved countless lives in surgery, received standing ovations, written important documents and provided affordable mental healthcare to three very disturbed schizophrenic teenagers.

nose to the chalkboard

Pretending to be asleep, I lay on my thin, rag rug waiting for naptime to be over. We were only in our kindergarten class for three hours a day, but Mrs. Morton, nearly seventy, believed strongly in a curriculum which included plenty of rest. How I coveted the cushioning power of rubber and fluff under Lisa Petronelli as she reclined on her fuzzy pink bathmat like a pampered Pomeranian.

Singing around the piano, bringing stuffed animals in for "Show and Tell"—eventually the mind begins to soften. Looking for subtle ways to add pleasure to our days, I parted my hair, and that of my friends, on the opposite side. We staggered around the room, enjoying the lopsided decadence of feeling slightly off balance and tipsy while Mrs. Morton looked on, befuddled.

When Mrs. Morton announced the beginning of story time, we gathered on the large braided rug. I was basically a good student, but induced by too much relaxation and "fairy-tale boredom," I was drawn to the dark side of misbehavior. One can only count dots in ceiling tiles and suck on loose strands of hair for so long before inventing a new form of entertainment, and that day what I happened upon was the art of donut-making. Surprisingly a knee sock, when carefully rolled down the leg, makes a lovely ring about the ankle. Whispers flew from one side of the story rug to the other, and soon all kindergarten-girl eyes were admiring my donut adornments. Within seconds the class broke into a hushed donut-making frenzy. Mrs. Morton, recognizing a shift in the mood of her audience, looked up from the pages of Hansel and Gretel to find that her story time had become something of a Pillsbury bakeoff. Without much trouble she was able to pick me out as the instigator leaning helpfully over my fellow confectioners, advising them of the importance of a good tight start. I was sent to the chalkboard to leave my nose print among the chalk dust with the other kindergarten criminals of the morning. Thus began my life of tempered disobedience in the public school system.

That summer, every soon-to-be first grader prayed passionate prayers hoping to be spared. "Please, dear God, don't let me get Mrs. Fate as my first grade teacher!" Mrs. Fate was the meanest teacher at Rockhill Elementary. Even fifth graders were afraid of running into her in the hall. Then the letter came, addressed "To the Parents of Ann Weimer." My mother, also fearful of a year with "The Fate worse than death," read the letter out loud, clasping her hands as she read, "Ann will be assigned to a split class of first and second graders with Mrs. Palloon." Mrs. Palloon! We'd never heard of her; she must be a new teacher. I bet she'd be pretty. Palloon rhymes with balloon; there was cause for hope.

On that first day of school when we met Mrs. Palloon, our

balloon of hope popped in one dreadful bang. Mrs. Fate had simply remarried over the summer and had a new last name. We were twenty-five victims trapped with a gray-haired screamer for an entire school year. I was so afraid of her that I didn't dream of misbehaving but moved rather to the art of poor attendance. Day after day of hearing my classmates vocally reamed out by our teacher was hard on me, and every few weeks I decided I'd earned a vacation. I'd ask to go to the nurse, saying I felt sick and needed to call my grandpa to come pick me up. Grandpa would walk down to the school to greet me and walk me to their house on Eastern Avenue, where he and Grandma would fill my afternoon with cheese curls, napping, and watching Grandma's programs until my mom got home from work.

In middle school, too big for the nose to the chalkboard form of discipline, I moved into "punishment of the pen." Perhaps this is where I picked up my love of writing. I had a creative French teacher who punished my playful antics in class by having me write, "I will not act like a dope in French class" 100 times. *Je ne serai pas bête dans la classe de français. Je ne serai pas bête dans la classe de français. Je ne serai pas bête dans la classe de français...*

In high school, when studying Van Gogh, I sent an ear in a box to my teacher, Mr. Sanders. It was really just a dried pear with ketchup and a note reading, "Ears to you! Sincerely, Vincent." (No one ever suspects the valedictorian.) Growing weary of Geometry and World History, I read paperbacks tucked behind the textbook. My inattention went undetected until I was reading a thriller by Steven King called *The Shining*. During a rather stressful chase scene I lost myself in the action and accidentally yelled out, "Run!" After the teacher and the class had a good laugh at me, I was given a pink slip—my first detention. It wasn't all bad. I met a whole new subset of people I hadn't come across in my classes. One such character was Ivan who took me under his wing describing what all the drugs looked like—purple haze, acid and others. He made me promise never to try them but wouldn't go so far as to give them up himself.

Even when I didn't mean to be, I was a disrupter of class. When something strikes me as funny, a solitary hiccup escapes. My sister calls it the hiccup of approval; she suffers from it too. It's where something is funny, but not quite deserving of a full laugh. I was sent to the hall in high school several times when that solo hiccup got the class laughing, and their appreciation of my "good form" brought on a storm of many more. In my family, a hiccup is not something that can be easily suppressed. Unlike others who swallow them with a residual tremor, ours are impossible to hold in and are unmercifully loud. It's kind of a family disability— some missing genetic material on the 46th chromosome which also causes us to sneeze whenever we step out into sunshine.

I carried these abnormalities into my adult life, and once during a lunch break at an all-day conference in Seattle, I challenged my coworker to see who could keep a pickle slice in her cheek the longest. After several hours of sitting through various lectures, we came together for dinner, where I proudly produced my limp slice—gone white after hours of soaking—only to find that Karen had chewed hers after the first ten minutes.

Karen and I both have daughters now, and it's interesting to see how our traits show up in our girls. My Emily enjoys making a little mischief like her mother. We put on our British accents at the grocery store as we pretend we're "on holiday visiting my mum in the States." We practice yodeling in the car and make up goofy song lyrics, but the other day Emily surprised me when she announced with great indignation at one of my scheme suggestions, "I will not be an 'accompanist' to your crimes!" Maybe my little accomplice is developing superior judgment and will be better able to keep her nose off the chalkboard. One can only hope.

photographs
pictures of my family

the three of us

Erich modeling Crayola's
fall collection

Ann, Erich, and Emily

Ann as "Miss Piggy"

Erich and Ann

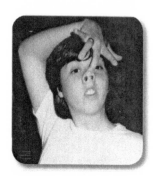

Along came our
daughter Emily

and like her dad,
watched the birds...

She blossomed...

Thank goodness they
didn't stick!

and made funny faces.

my grandparents

Ann and Mom wearing party hats,
kissing a reluctant Nana on her birthday.

Another birthday—another kiss.
Jen and I prepared a fancy lunch
in the backyard for Nana.

Grandma and Grandpa striking a pose
like the one in the picture behind them.

Grandma tried on Jen's bib overalls and hiking boots.

my parents

Dad—always a bridesmaid, never a bride.

Mom warming up...

Dad being Dad

A mirrored wall makes
Mom's outstretched arm and
leg look pretty impressive.

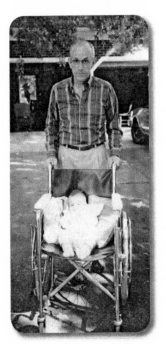

Dad taking Emily
for her first ride in the wheelchair

Mom jumping rope
with my cousin's kids.

sisters

Jennifer and Ann

Jen in the crib with
Emily and Elaine

Jen pushing my tricycle

Emily, Elaine, Ann and Jen in
"The Two Little Pigs"

Ann, Uncle Walt, Dad, and
Jen showing off aluminum foil
Father's Day ties

Ann, Mom, and Jen dressed
to kill for a "murder drama"
with the neighbors

our girls

Elaine, Meg, and Emily

Super Meg

Loving ya like a sister

Meg under cover

Acting in the back of the van

On Frozen Pond

Emily, Meg, and Elaine
at a Yankees game

Elaine, Meg, and Emily

curtain call

H.R.H. Ann

My brother-in-law, Kevin

Our most recent family portrait where we all
mysteriously turned up looking like Dad.

Lights out for Dad—
with a quick nap on a footstool.

My parents' garage doubles
as a summer porch.

Neighbors stop by for a chat.

snip and tuck

I was going through our box of "dud photos" to see if there might be some funny ones I could cut up and put on a get well card for my mom. You may be shocked to hear I would even consider breaking the sanctity of a photograph by chopping bits out, but I come from a tradition where no photo is safe from scissor OR pen.

As I trimmed around the blond curly edges of my daughter's "bed head," trying carefully to include every fly-away piece of hair, I remembered how my mother once mailed snapshots of their vacation to my aunt and uncle in California. Included in the collection was a photo of the four of them standing on my aunt and uncle's boat, enjoying a pleasant afternoon on the lake. Everyone's eyes were open, their smiles just right, and the wind was being kind to hairstyles. In my mother's eyes the only thing ruining that picture was the profile of her stomach. She grabbed her sewing scissors and in minutes had corrected the flaw by cutting a small hole in the picture where her tummy used to be. Now she was satisfied. Where others might go to great lengths and expensive surgeries to remove an unwanted bulge, my mother did it with her own scissors in a matter of minutes without messy scars or risks of infection.

It isn't to say that Mom didn't worry about her profile when she caught a glimpse in the mirror. She wasn't happy with her shape, so she set out to do something about it. Mom was a teacher and "hip" to motivational techniques, so for years we had graph paper on our refrigerator charting her morning weight. And when you opened the cookie jar, you'd find a grease-soaked note yelling a warning in bold magic marker, "Don't do it!" To appeal to the visual learner, mom drew a stick figure with a protruding stomach on the lid of the butter tub. Sometimes these encouragements of Mom's were difficult to navigate around, and you'd end up having to explain it all to friends when they'd ask, "Why do you have a picture of a pregnant person on your butter?" What they didn't know was that there were matching sets on the ice cream and the nut tin as well.

Since I was never sure what I'd find taped to our goodies at home, I often suggested to friends that we go to Grandma's house to see what she had. Unlike my mother, who had just one problem area, my grandmother was riddled with them. The difference was that Grandma didn't care. Grandma was so comfortable with her figure, in fact, that she let me play with the flab under her arms, allowing me to poke and jiggle as long as I wanted. I liked laying my cheek against it feeling the coolness of that loose skin with my face. I longed for the day when I could have flab of my own. Nobody in Grandma's house was interested in losing weight because my grandmother loved to bake, and Grandpa had a sweet tooth. He loved Grandma's cooking, but if she didn't have something ready, he'd just drink sugar water until it was time for the cookies to come out of the oven.

My mother has always had a nice figure, and as long as she could stay motivated and away from the temptations at Grandma's, she did pretty well. But sometimes success requires additional strategic maneuvers from the family. My dad's first line of defense is always "search and destroy." He sets out to eat as much of the offending food as possible and pass it off to guests to get it out of the house. After that he moves into camouflage mode. For Christmas this year someone gave my parents a big tin of nuts. After an evening with the cashews in her lap, Mom turned them over to Dad and with unusual honesty confessed, "George, you're going to need to find some new hiding places. I'm onto your old ones." After forty-one years of living in the same house, it's increasingly difficult for my dad to find new hiding places, but I know that with his stealth knowledge and practiced eye, he'll be able to provide protection from whatever may befall them—be it cashews, Fritos or other calorie-ridden dangers.

the cable guy's serenade

"Now just reboot your computer and we'll see if that fixed it." The cable technician on the phone, stepping me through my computer e-mail problems, was so patient and helpful. But as my computer slowly chugged and ticked back to life again, we found ourselves in one of those black holes, suffering through awkward silence. On a whim I asked the technician if he'd mind singing some elevator music to get us through the seemingly endless, uncomfortable moment as we waited for my computer to restart. I expected a polite chuckle, but without answering, my cable guy erupted into song... "Jeremiah was a bullfrog! Nah Nah Nah. Was a good friend of mine. Nah Nah Nah. Never understood a single word he said, but I helped him drink his wine."

Through the receiver I could hear the chuckling of his office mates, but my cable guy continued undaunted, only breaking in at one point to defend himself, saying, "She asked for this. I'm just providing good customer service." Before the serenade ended my computer had restarted, and we were back diagnosing the last remaining problems. At my final reboot and extended silence, I didn't even have to ask; my ever-thoughtful cable guy seamlessly moved from conversation into song and switching genres, began twittering in Julie Andrews falsetto, "The hills are alive with the sound of muuuusic. Ahh. Ahh. Ahh. Ahh."

I've often wondered if the cable company happened to record our jammin' help session to train other cable operators in the fine art of providing good customer service, but since then, in all my hours being stuck on the phone with telephone operators, no one has yet offered to sing me elevator music quite like that.

Reprinted from Christian Science Monitor March 17, 2005

monkey for the middle

I have always been a person after the center whether it's the soft middle of bread, the heart of the watermelon, or the center of attention. I can't help myself; I'm a monkey for the middle. For high school graduation, while others asked for trips to Europe, luggage, or cars, I asked if I could eat the heart and only the heart out of a whole watermelon. Anyone who loves watermelon knows what I'm talking about; the heart is the very best part. In the days before seedless melons, it was the only piece you could count on being absolutely free of those woody black seeds. My mother and I would shamelessly shave bits of heart until the watermelon's concave center smiled so deeply it gave us away.

Now I'm supposed to bring a sheet cake for a church fundraiser. Do I bring lemon or chocolate? I can't decide, so I make both. I love them—lemon and chocolate—equally and desperately.

I sit with the two cakes I love best, alone in the house for hours. I ice them while they're still warm enough to make the icing go a bit drippy. My chocolate cake... My lemon cake...

"You know," I say to myself, "these sheet cakes are going to be cut into squares and handed out to people; it won't hurt if I cut a piece from each for myself. It's probably a good practice anyway, just to be sure the cake is good." Not only do I want a piece of cake, I want the center piece. The one at the absolute height of the cake. The moistest one with no dry, low-lying edges.

The screen door slams; my husband and daughter are home. I have this "uh-oh feeling." But why should I be scared? I'm the mom! Emily and Erich look at the sheet cakes with horror and shock. "How did you get that out of there?" my husband asks. Extreme desire makes one precise. No surgeon could've excised a tumor from a temporal lobe with as much care.

"You're not going to take them like THAT to the church, are you?" Erich wonders.

"It won't hurt anything," I pipe back, "It's the new bundt."

my mother can't swim

My mother can't swim. It's strange to see your mom gaspy and mechanical as she tries to learn the strokes. She can't swim, but I know if I were drowning, she would jump in to save me. We'd most likely drown together, but somehow it's nice to have the company. Other mothers would call for help, grab a pole, a life preserver—something to make themselves useful, but my mom has passion and would run to me, shoes and all. It's wonderful to have a person in your life who loves you beyond logic. You want to draw her close and protect her from her passion—the thing you most love about her and most fear.

the baked potato cure

I can't tell you how tired I am of heating up the old baked potato for another fifteen minute "sit" on my eye. "You have what's called a chalazion, (ka LAZY an)" the doctor said. "a blocked oil gland on your eyelid." How many months ago was that? The lancing didn't make it go away, so we're back to a hot baked potato twice a day. At first it was a novelty. Once off the eye, I ate them with bacon and cheddar cheese. Then my pants got too tight, and I had to change my methods to simply reheat the same potato over and over again. Soon the potato skin grew brittle and flaked. My friends would find bits of spud on my face the way someone graciously tells you that you have spinach in your teeth. Of course I felt I had to explain why potato bits were caught in my eyebrows—not quite the usual place for food to get lodged.

Now I've got an itchy place on my lower eyelid; another one is coming. Why am I getting all these chalazions? I had never even heard of them before. My hairdresser said, "Isn't Chalazion a book of the Bible?" Can't you just hear a minister saying, "Now let's turn to Second Chalazions, chapter 3..." The doctor says this might be an allergic response to our cat. He said I should wash my eyelids every night with Johnson's baby shampoo, use special eye drops three times a day, and keep going with the hot potato. When I complained, he suggested dry rice in a sock as an alternative. I was objecting to the thirty minutes a day, not the lack of variety in food eye patches. Nevertheless I decided to give rice, "the other starch" a try but found it didn't hold the heat as well as a potato. Unfortunately, in trying to superheat the rice in the microwave, I overcooked it, and the house smelled like burned popcorn for two days. I hope to soon be rid of my double chalazions, but something tells me we haven't heard the last of it yet. I'll keep you posted.

my satchel

What would you call it? It's not really a purse because I don't wear it on my shoulder or carry it in my hand. Although I wear it around my waist, I wouldn't call it a fanny pack. It doesn't have that distinctive "click-lock" mechanism on all things campy. I decided this *thing* I put together from several items on the clearance rack should be called my *satchel*. An old word nobody really uses or knows what it means. A lot like fortnight or breakfront.

My satchel is big enough to hold a wallet, keys and a tissue. It has a huge white "R" standing boldly on its black faux-leather background. "What does the "R" stand for?" everyone always wants to know. It would be handy if my name started with an "R", but since it doesn't, I like to come up with answers that fit my mood. Sometimes I say, "The 'R' stands for writer." Other times I'll ask them what they think the "R" could be. My husband said, "Radiant!" I'll have to freeze frame that moment for the next time he forgets our anniversary. "Radical!" says my Republican father-in-law. "Rascal!" says my daughter and nieces who know me too well. "Raving lunatic! Ridiculous!" offers my ever-helpful sister who would never dream of carrying such a thing.

Wearing an "R" that changes meaning with my moods makes sense to me. I always have something to spark two minutes of interesting conversation in an elevator or grocery store line. And my satchel goes nicely with my Native American earrings, which have three Indian symbols carved into the silver, meaning who knows what? I've lost the paper telling the true translation, so when people ask what they mean, I make it up. Some days its "earth, wind, and fire" other days, "rock, paper, scissors." It's nice to have such a versatile wardrobe that, like a 1970's mood ring, morphs with me from minute to minute.

dove love

You may have heard all the hoopla in the media lately about the way flavonoids have a protective effect on heart function. Remarkably, foods rich in flavonoids are not the expected noxious brussels sprouts but instead include grape juice, red wine and chocolate. Grape juice is a controlled substance in our house because of its pervasive staining power, so in the interest of protecting my heart with the recommended daily allowance of flavonoids, I've been eating a lot more chocolate these days.

Since our health insurance doesn't cover prescriptions for Godiva, Lindt and Dolfin, I've been forced into eating ChapStick-like American chocolate, so waxy that if you were to light the confetti-paper wick on a Hershey's kiss, you could enjoy nearly 20 minutes of ambient light.

After much research—and I do mean much—I've found Dove bars to be my medicine of choice. A side effect of taking Dove bars "b.i.d." (that's twice daily in pharmacy language) is that you amass a large collection of foil wrappers with poetic sayings inside. I started out with light chocolate but moved to dark after hearing that dark chocolate has a higher concentration of flavonoids. Interestingly, I've found the dark chocolate "sayings" to be more seductive than the light chocolate ones. Just the other day I saw "Naughty can be nice." "Hey, why not?" and "Temptation can be fun." Now my husband and I take part in "Dove Love." Instead of buying flowers or writing love notes to one another, we simply exchange Dove wrappers as we watch *NYPD Blue* reruns. If you need a way to spice up your marriage and at that same time promote good health, I suggest you come to the dark side and self-prescribe Dove bars. You'll be glad you did.

hair on my chest

I have hair on my chest—not necessarily a bad thing, except that I'm a forty-one-year-old woman. The hair isn't mine; it's Benny's. It appears he loses great clouds of fur during his springtime thaw. Before I leave the house, I frisk myself with enormous tape curls. Our cat's previous owners assured us this extreme hair loss is a temporary thing that will self-correct in a few months. We've agreed to pet ownership on a trial basis.

When my husband proposed, we didn't sign a pre-nup. Instead, we had a discussion in which he agreed to certain conditions. He had to promise not to pressure me or make me feel bad about not having a pet. Eighteen years later he found a loophole in our thirteen-year-old daughter who pressured me and made me feel bad for not having a pet. We started with a gerbil that to this day I've never touched. I talk to it through the glass and throw in gerbil chow when Emily's at camp. I've learned from other people's pets that lunging, licking, barking and biting means they want to play. I'm awkward with animals. I'm all right unless I have to pick them up. There's no good handle; they're all legs and unprotected organs. I go so far as to make kissing noises to Benny, and if he doesn't come, well then, it just wasn't meant to be.

There is a part of me that really loves Benny. I hold him in the morning while I'm checking e-mail. He lies in my arms like a baby with his head in the crook of my elbow while he paws the air. When replying to messages, I write back capless responses because I can't use my other hand to hold down the shift key. I try to hold him three times a day for ten to fifteen minutes. We're satisfied with this arrangement. On days when I wear black and have de-furred already, I tiptoe around answering the phone on the first ring, hoping not to waken him. Fortunately he sleeps a lot. I called his "real" mom to ask for advice on removing eye boogers and to see if he might be sick because he sleeps so much. She assured me that it's all normal.

Once a cat senses you're beginning to fall in love with him, he tests your devotion by leaving a mess somewhere in your house. We had a close call last week. I called my mother-in-law, a licensed bird rehabilitator, saying I needed her help with an animal rescue situation. I proceeded to tell her that the cat had made a diarrhea mess on the carpet, and if he were to continue to survive, I needed to know how one goes about removing that from a rug. Grandma's vinegar and cornmeal trick worked. Benny was spared; he's still got all nine lives left.

t. rex

I have this coat. It's long, black and beautiful. A "find" from the Goodwill for twenty dollars. It's a vintage winter coat from the 1940's with an oversized collar that when flipped up and held at your chin, encircles your face like the petals of a flower.

When I wear my coat, I'm exotic; I'm Marilyn Monroe; I'm Audrey Hepburn. I hear the flash bulbs of the Paparazzi, my bodyguards moving me to my limo. I'm waving to my fans, and then... like the tear of a needle across a record album, it all ends.

Herein lies the fatal flaw to this coat. The arms. For some reason, the sleeves were cut wrong; the armpits are nowhere near your armpits but come more from the area of your waistline so I find myself unable to lift my arms beyond half mast. Like the tiny helpless dinosaur arms of *Tyrannosaurus rex*, I can just wiggle them ineffectually from side to side.

I can't drive, can't wave, can't even get my arms up high enough to put my seat belt on. If someone gives me a hug, I return with a passionless nothing—my arms pinned to my sides. You might say, "Why would anyone wear such a coat?" And the answer is, of course... "Because it's JUST... THAT... GORGEOUS."

Reprinted from Christian Science Monitor March 7, 2005

long distance decorating

My mom lives 250 miles away and was trying to get my help in choosing between two carpet samples I've never seen. She's very verbal and has a wonderful vocabulary, but over the phone how do you accurately describe subtle differences between a beige carpet and a beige carpet? I'm proud to announce, however, that after twenty minutes of back and forth, I think I finally convinced her to go with the beige one.

al dente

Instead of my usual galloping down the stairs, I gingerly made my way—arms crossed on my chest to provide support for my budding teenaged breasts.

"Mom, will they always be this sore?"

"Oh, no," my mother said convincingly, "Eventually they'll feel just like an arm or a leg. You'll hardly even know they're there."

She was right. Eventually they stopped hurting, but as for an arm or a leg, I'm not so sure. Although I've tried to support them over the years with wires and bras that promise to "lift and separate," I doubt they'll be strong enough to carry me into my old age when my knees finally give out. When I was a new mother, they did come in handy at feeding time but weren't much good when it came to changing diapers. And I've noticed the digits at the ends of my arms and legs don't seem to stand at attention at a cool breeze the way the others do. No. They don't hurt anymore, but I must say, mine have never quite achieved arm or leg status. Maybe I just haven't tried hard enough or spent enough time in training, but you'd think with my initial sensitivity to motion, I would've welcomed the support of a bra. Not me. Like a wild pony, I've never taken well to the saddle.

The straps were never quite right—always too tight or too loose. They'd either wander out my sleeve and down my arm like those of the old ladies who sat in front of me in church or they'd cut off blood supply—making my fingers go numb. I could think of nothing all day but the fact that I was wearing a bra, feeling every inch of cotton and elastic conspiring to strangle me.

My mom suggested I wear it for an hour at a time or buy a 44 double A (which doesn't exist, by the way—I checked) just to have the "lines" of a bra for society's sake. But eventually I succumbed to America's pressure and my mother's insistence on wearing the thing. I was broken.

Then, years later, came a hot, humid vacation in Florida with my husband. My distemper with the bra once again returned, only this time to a more lenient trainer than my mother. Like the horse whisperer, Erich didn't want to break my wild spirit. "Let the girl run free" was his motto. He was more than thrilled with the idea of my going bareback. When on a hot and sweaty hike I suggested removing the contraption, he answered me with cheers. "By all means, take it off." To his delight I did the trick all women know, where you make some Houdini moves—dislocating a shoulder here, compressing your backbone there—and voila; like a rabbit out of a hat, I pulled my bra out from my sleeve.

Wondrous! Fantastic! Remarkable! This newfound feeling of freedom deserved a word or a song or something. I coined the phrase 'al dente' to mean going bra-less. Later, at the hotel, when we'd finally decided on a restaurant for dinner, I asked Erich, "How do you feel about me going al dente tonight?" I know "al dente" is an Italian word having something to do with the "doneness" of a noodle, but this lovely condition of bra-less-ness needed a foreign word as a descriptor. No English phrase was beautiful or exotic enough to express the feeling. I enjoyed going 'al dente' so much that I pretty much spent the whole vacation in that mode. I can tell you there was much anguish when I returned to civilization and had to go back to wearing the bra for an hour at a time, starting the whole training process over again.

southern michigan

Southern Michigan... You're sure it's called southern Michigan because southern Michigan sounds nothing like the name of a Chinese dish. Did it come with rice, or was it served with noodles?"

My neighbor-friend and I take walks every day for exercise, free therapy, and mindless chit-chat. But today we were wading deep in the soggy corners of my brain, trying to figure out what southern Michigan had to do with Chinese food.

I'm one of those people who think in pictures as a way to remember things. Information goes in just fine, but when I try to retrieve it, it comes out a little different. For instance, when I try to recover the well-known phrase, "He's always putting his two cents in," I get the picture right, but the words wrong with: "He's the kind who wants to put his two pennies in." My sister Jennifer has lived with me long enough that she can usually figure out these puzzlers, but she's six hundred miles away and not much help at the moment.

In college, when Jen and I drove from Ohio to Seattle to visit our cousin, we kept ourselves awake listing state capitals. We worked our way alphabetically through the states until we came to South Dakota. No city name was coming to me, but a picture was forming in my mind. I saw frothy, bubbling water. "White water! Something with white water!" I yelled.

"Rapid City!" my sister fired back. Now, Rapid City was indeed the name of the town I was thinking of; unfortunately it is *not* the capital of South Dakota. The capital of South Dakota is Pierre. Pierre... what a funny name... It makes me think of a French poodle with a ridiculous bow on his tail. Now the next time I'm asked to come up with the capital of South Dakota I'll have a good laugh at myself when I say, "A male poodle. For some reason I'm thinking of France... and a male poodle..."

If you're wondering, my neighbor and I finally came up with the solution to our southern Michigan dilemma. The name of the Chinese dish was...can you guess? Lo Mein. I got my "M" states confused and substituted Michigan for Maine. As for Lo, everyone knows that on a map, south is always the lowest position. If you're beginning to follow my logic, then please drop me a line. I'm in the market for a local interpreter.

leaning into the groove

My husband was gone on a business trip. I was standing in line at a Roly Poly sandwich shop when I found myself leaning my head dangerously close to the back of the man in front of me. I love to put my head in the groove of my husband's back when he's standing over the stove, frying his weekly pound of bacon. That gentle ditch of bone and flesh between his shoulder blades that holds my head "just so." I called my husband in Minneapolis that night and told him he needed to get home fast, as I had almost leaned into another man's groove. He suggested we get a cat.

I thought the cat would be good for me as I hit my forties and moved into this strange period where I needed so much more affection. When my friend hit forty, she told her husband, "Either we get a dog or I find a lover. You pick." They got a dog. My daughter is a teenager, and my husband is a forty-two year old man into computer games and online poker. Nobody has time for me. Nobody, except the cat, who wants me almost constantly. It's one of those situations where the cure becomes the next problem. Now I find myself tiptoeing around the house hoping not to waken my feline stalker, who searches me out like a heat-seeking missile.

My neighbor called me the other day to tell me cats have been known to live thirty years; she's just full of good news. But I laughed at her when they got a second dog, a puppy who cries every night and needs to pee at five a.m. A few hours later our cat's clawless feet paw frantically at our bedroom door longing for body heat and flannel sheets. When his pawing doesn't work, he lies down and sticks one arm under the door all the way up to his armpit. It's pathetic to have something want you that badly.

Now I know how my family feels when I open my arms and assume the "hug me, PLEASE" position. As I draw energy from an embrace, these introverts I live with make sucking noises as if their life force is being drained from them. They disengage from the hug, wobbling to their respective computers to revive themselves with instant messaging and playing poker with strangers. Where's the cat? I need some lovin' fast! What's wrong with women in their forties? Why do we feel so desperate for affection? I guess we'll manage though as long as our pets stay healthy, our husbands don't take long business trips, and the men in front of us wear bulky sweaters to protect their groove.

the wisdom of a full stop

Knowing when to stop is an important life skill. I'm not just talking about the obvious times like stop signs and red lights, I'm talking about breakfast at Perkins. You have an order of eggs, toast, and another plate set aside for your triple tier of pancakes. You're doing fine, moving through the breakfast fare, when "BAM!" you suddenly hit the wall with your pancakes. A pancake wall is nothing to mess with; when you hit it, respect the wall and put that pancake down. I don't care if it's your last bite. With pancakes there's no forgiveness factor like you have with other foods. Respect the wall.

Another time you must come to a full stop is when you develop goose bumps in the middle of shaving your legs. Unfortunately, I've learned this lesson several times. The last and final time I disobeyed this safety rule, it was wintertime. The season of long pants, long pants that with each move tear the tender miniature scabs off the thousands of evenly spaced headless goose bumps up and down your legs. Whether I'm shaving for a summer picnic or a swim in the pool, I always bring my razor to a screeching halt at the first sign of a goose bump.

In my younger days I used to be able to ignore the early warnings of a full bladder. I called them remissions, where you might go several hours before having to stop what you were doing to take care of business. Now I'm in my forties, and urinary remissions are a thing of the past. I've never been one to enjoy exercise. I know Kegel exercises could be done without even breaking a sweat, but when the gynecologist suggested after the birth of our daughter that I do them at every red light FOR THE REST OF MY LIFE, I rebelled. I guess I'm paying the price for my reckless nature. If I had done those stoplight exercises, perhaps my heart rate would be lower, I might have less plaque in my arteries, and certainly my sphincter muscles would be in better shape. Maybe I could have avoided bringing my life to a full stop each time I hear rain on the roof or put my hands in dishwater, but sometimes life's wisdom comes a little late.

the macgyver gene

Have you ever seen that TV show called "MacGyver," where the main character is able to free himself from prison, restore the brakes in a runaway vehicle, and save a child from a burning building using nothing more than a toothpick, pocket fuzz, and a wrapper from a Big Mac?

Although my family's name is Weimer, we somehow turned out to have a bit of the "MacGyver" in us. From my dad and sister to my uncles and cousins, we have our own unique way of solving problems. One day I called my sister on the phone. We both have headsets like the real operators do, so we can be mobile while we talk and have our hands free. Jen told me she was ironing, but I kept hearing outside noises like cars going by and the sound of kids riding big wheels on the driveway.

"Where ARE you?" I asked.

"I'm ironing in the front yard. It's too nice of a day to be shut inside. That's what those orange extension cords are for anyway, isn't it?"

Only my sister, the multi-tasker, would think of a way to get the ironing done while talking to her sister, while watching the kids play outside, while getting a tan.

My cousin Jerry also inherited the "MacGyver gene" and is very resourceful when it comes to solving problems. He's a contractor working side by side on projects with his eighty-year-old dad, my uncle Bob. You'd think at eighty, my uncle would be slowing down, but construction work has always kept him in great shape. One hot Montana afternoon, Jerry and Uncle Bob were busy at a remote site putting a new roof on a building when Uncle Bob mysteriously slumped over unconscious. Jerry is a volunteer firefighter and quickly got to him, checking his heart rate and breathing. It appeared Uncle Bob had passed out from too much blood-pressure medicine. Jerry could not waken him, and since no one was around, Jerry knew he had to go get help.

Now for the dilemma. How to keep my uncle from rolling off the roof while Jerry was gone? Jerry reached for his hammer and his pouch of roofing tacks while kneeling gingerly beside Uncle Bob. Like a life-sized version of a connect-the-dots picture, Jerry systematically anchored his dad to the roof with nails driven every few inches through Uncle Bob's flannel shirt and baggy jean coveralls. Grabbing the loose fabric and cinching it with roofing tacks, Jerry eventually pinned his dad around the perimeter of his body until each arm and leg was securely fastened to the roof. If Uncle Bob "came to" while Jerry was gone, all he'd be able to do would be to lift his head, wiggle his feet and whistle.

Since their harrowing rooftop experience, Uncle Bob has been grounded to projects no higher than five feet off the ground.

Unfortunately the shirt couldn't be saved, as it started to unravel after the first laundering, but Uncle Bob still wears his coveralls; he calls them his "dot-to-dots."

perfectly flawed

Emily has had braces on her teeth for almost two years now. While we were back at the orthodontist's for our monthly "after-school tune-up," I lamented to Dr. Denver about how straight Emily's teeth were getting.

"Straight!" he said, "Well, of course they're getting straight! That's what we wanted them to do. That's why you paid me four thousand dollars."

"Yes, I know, but did you have to make them sooo straight? My daughter smiles at me with the mouth of a stranger; I want my Emily back!"

"Too late," Dr. Denver said. "She's perfect, and there's nothing I can do about it."

"Well," I replied, "At least I still have the scar in her eyebrow."

I can't help it; I happen to like the little imperfections in people. The twists in my grandmother's crooked fingers, the way my husband can snap his toes. It's these physical flaws of nature— the beauty marks, the love handles, and the occasional scar—that give us character anyway.

We should be proud of our scars. They often represent daring achievements, or at least attempts at daring achievements. Years ago, I made up a game I called "Scar Search." It was born, like most of my ideas, out of boredom on a long car ride. Each of us took turns being judges—grading, not only the impressiveness of someone's scar, but also the story that went along with it. I won "best story" when I told about falling backwards onto a paring knife as the dishwasher drawer lay open. Ten points for the story, but zero for the scar, since I refused to drop my pants to show it. We learned more about each other in that hour than in months of casual friendship. Don't be so quick to tuck your tummy; your true friends will actually miss it.

miracle on willow drive

I've never had that born-again experience some Christians go through, but I've had something close. Last week was the first time we had a cleaning lady come to our house. I've been gasping and sputtering all week, unable to find words to express my joy.

No longer can I say, "You can eat off our floor and get a pretty well-balanced meal." Gone are the stray peas that rolled out of the bag and into far-off corners. Gone is the soy milk puddle Emily wiped up in that kid way, where the milk is gone but the stickum remains behind.

The kitchen floor has lost its ring-around-the-collar dinge after years of only getting "just so close" before the sponge mop bumped into the baseboards. The toaster no longer drops bread crumbs like Hansel and Gretel across the countertops. Everything shines. Life is good. Yes, Virginia, there is a Santa Claus.

i'm the grown-up

I'm the grown-up. Sometimes I forget this and slip back into old habits I had as a child, habits like making my bed for a mother who now lives hundreds of miles away. What freedom when my husband and I both discovered that neither one of us cared whether or not we slept in a "made" bed. So now we don't make it; haven't for five years. Those first thirteen years of our marriage are lost to us, but just think of all the unmade beds we have in our future!

This grown-upness counts in parenting too. Although I felt like an unfit mother the first time I did it, I eventually got used to dressing our toddler in her clothes for the next day instead of having her wear pajamas. Those soft cotton pants and t-shirts were the same as pajamas anyway. Who could tell the difference? I figured I might as well start the next day with one thing already checked off my to-do list. Dressed for the day? Check!

I'm not the most traditional grown-up either when it comes to birthdays. Emily has never been fond of cake, so one year I gave her a tub of lemon icing with candles in it. Another year I carried a flaming watermelon half into a roomful of five-year-olds, singing "Happy Birthday." After cutting up birthday watermelon we played "find the phone," which I would hide and they would find by listening for the beeping when we pressed the "locator" button. As you might imagine, I don't like to bother with the fine trappings of ribbons and wrapping paper. I've discovered that with aluminum foil, you just drape it over the present and squeeze. Voila! You have a wrapped present that sparkles and is totally recyclable.

Even before kids can tell time their inner clock sets off alarms at the toughest part of the day, when you're trying to make supper. To make things easier, I screwed the backyard swing into the ceiling of our kitchen so I could keep an eye on Emily as she swang, sang, and chatted with me while I chopped vegetables. The retired neighbor lady across the street could see us in the window and called to see what was going on. She said, "I see feet, and then I don't see feet."

As much fun as it can be to be nontraditional, there are times where convention rules. Let's face it; brushing your teeth is a pretty good practice and actually feels kind of good. You can't have Pop-Tarts for supper... every night. And if you put off the laundry for too long, it becomes a problem. Luckily, with our "Big House" operation of playing prison with the neighbor kids, we not only get the socks folded but can also check off another task. So much for convention...Laundry? Check!

i'm no martha stewart

N o one will ever confuse me with Martha Stewart. Just last week I burned a batch of boiled eggs and in the process turned my Revere pan purple. I used to be a molecular geneticist working with DNA sequencing gels, monoclonal antibodies and other impressive, hard-to-spell words. It sounds wonderful, but basically all I did was follow scientific recipes using ingredients that could kill me. "Cooking with radiation" is what I lovingly called it. Let's just say it's in the nation's best interest that I changed careers and am no longer in the laboratory.

We have a tradition in my family of burning food. My mom once left a ham cooking in the oven overnight. We ate it. That's what you did back then; you didn't waste food. We had to cut away about three inches of charred meat, but the inside was some of the best ham I've ever tasted.

My Nana used only two settings on her electric stovetop, off and high. Her fried eggs were seared—curled and burned to a nice crisp. I started using ketchup on my eggs to cover the carbon flavor but then got hooked because it was Nana's home brew made from her own garden tomatoes. Nana preserved her ketchup in little glass Coke bottles. I never got over the thrill of watching her pop off the metal soda lid with a bottle opener and pouring the sweet-red-tomatoey mess in a puddle for dipping.

Although burning things is a family legacy, there is, however, one thing I make quite well—Grandma Weimer's ginger cookies. I'm the only one in the family who is willing to work with less flour and put up with their stickiness in order to get that plump little belly in the center that's soft and cake-like. Ginger cookies are so frustrating that I rarely make them. Last year for Christmas I wrote to a good friend and told her that IF I'd made ginger cookies, she would've gotten some. She was duly impressed and felt honored to have been on the short list of those who WOULD'VE received cookies. Because they're such a hassle to make, my dad offered to help me one time, but we accidentally sprinkled them with salt instead of sugar. My long-gone grandma came to the rescue as we used her bread knife to decapitate the salty tops from the now somewhat-edible bottoms. Although I was to some extent spared from a complete cooking mishap, everyone who knows me is happy I'm not Martha Stewart. No one wants me too close to the kitchen.

shirley, you jest

My mom has very fine hair; it won't hold a curl. Not one to waste time, my mother has read thousand-page books while forcing curl into her hair each morning. Persistence pays off, and she comes out of the powder room both well-read and gorgeous.

Dad has fifty-two weeks of vacation and is always looking for things to do. He carefully times Mom's curling process so he can have her toast, tea, and morning collection of pills ready and perfectly synchronized with the last fogging of hair spray.

After breakfast one morning Mom went back in for some touch-up curl. When she returned to the kitchen, she found what looked like her oversized calcium pill cut in half on her placemat.

"Why would George cut my pill in half? He knows it's harder to swallow that way."

She poured herself a glass of water and downed the pill halves. A few minutes later Dad came into the kitchen looking for something he'd lost. He lifted each placemat and looked under the table.

"Shirley, have you seen those two little white caps that go on the end of our wire shelving? They were just here; I don't know what I did with them."

With a sick look on her face Mom answered, "How soon do you need them?"

the mark of a cheeto eater

You know who you are. I'm one too. We recognize each other by the unmistakable orange residue in the beds of our fingernails. You may think you've licked those fingers clean—erased all traces of fake cheese—but there's always a nook where that give-away orangeness gets stuck. When e-mailing friends, I type capless letters so I can fully dedicate one hand to delivering Cheetos rather than gum up the keys. They understand; they too are Cheeto lovers.

In an effort to keep my fingers from telling on me, I've taken to pouring Cheetos into my open mouth. This works well unless you're as uncoordinated as I am and get Cheeto dust all over your shirt. I went to work (three hours post-Cheeto), and a coworker found one intact in the folds of my turtleneck.

My sister ate so many Cheetos while she was pregnant that they nicknamed her growing bulge "Cheeto." Jen's husband was convinced with all that orange food coloring going in for nine months that the baby would surely come out with at least red hair and freckles, but as it turned out, their newborn wasn't even jaundiced.

Although Cheetoing is tough to hide, I guess there's no real reason to be ashamed. They ARE habit-forming, but as of yet they're not illegal or listed as a controlled substance. until the fda gets involved, i think i'll eat my cheetos with reckless abandon. i'm a cheeto eater, and i'm proud of it...i'd use an exclamation mark there, but it's difficult to do one-handed. you understand, right. question mark.

illegal substitution

Timeouts may have worked when she was a toddler, but as a teenager our daughter would like nothing better than to be sent to her room. Instead, our punishments involve having Emily perform some dreaded duty off our own to-do list. That's how Emily wound up making supper for us one Monday night.

I offered my services as helper, since this was Emily's first time cooking beyond scrambling an egg, but she was excited about doing it herself and wanted the dinner to be a surprise. She carefully set the table remembering napkins and candles. She paged through my recipe book deciding finally on some kind of chicken curry pasta. Unfortunately, we didn't have the right kind of pasta, so she boiled spaghetti noodles instead. We were out of chicken, but she found some slices of cold roast beef to lay on the steaming noodles. No curry? She'd simply have to make a substitution. Cinnamon—that ought to work. Our chicken curry pasta had morphed into a monstrous concoction of cold beef on spaghetti with cinnamon. Who was the one being punished here?

Because Emily was so proud of her first home-cooked dinner, Erich and I ate with grace and thanksgiving for our daughter who had so lovingly cooked this marvel for us—a dinner no five-star restaurant ever dared to attempt.

Recipes available upon request.

nomenclature

Our house looks like every other house on the street; boring—except for our yard full of dandelions. To "jazz" things up a bit, my daughter Emily and I have taken to naming things in exotic ways. We have a "Diving Board" in the kitchen (that half wall divider that separates the breakfast nook from the living room) and we cook on a "Peninsula" (it's a lot like an island, but one end of the counter is attached to a major land mass—the sink). We watch television in the "Ladies' Sitting Room" named mostly because we wanted to hear my husband Erich say "Ladies' Sitting Room." Our foyer has a table I call the "Breakfront" because my Nana used to put pennies on the breakfront of her hutch and I wanted that word in my life. Erich resists these exotic locations in the house and is opposed to our use of intentional misnomers. "It's not a diving board!" he forever instructs.

Grandma Tildy arrived on our doorstep a few years ago. She was a gift from my sister; an enormous body pillow for me to hug to help my sore back. Emily and I named the pillow after a favorite character in a book. For those who don't know Grandma Tildy, they might be shocked to hear me giving Emily instructions on laundry day, "Emily, Grandma Tildy's a bit bent out of shape and weak in the knees. Will you knock the stuffing out of her before you dress her in her clean outfit?" With the practiced technique of a professional wrestler, Emily lifts Grandma Tildy high over her head and body slams her with a few well-placed karate chops to redistribute her flab and love handles. Then Emily shoves Grandma Tildy headfirst into the pillowcase and bounces her into position.

Erich corrects us whenever we refer to Grandma Tildy as a "her" and will probably never forgive my sister for this added hassle in his life. Emily and I have been celebrating a small victory we had recently. Although he denies it, Erich accidentally used the pronoun "her" instead of "it" when referring to Grandma Tildy. "Must we take 'her' on every vacation and weekend trip?" he complained. Like most grandmothers, Grandma Tildy is soft and pliable (she can nearly bend in half), but she definitely presents packing problems for a midsized car.

Initially, in my effort to make travel more convenient, I searched the web for a blow up body pillow, but trust me…you don't want to go there. Eventually though, I came up with a solution I call Travel Tildy. Rather than packing the pillow itself, I bring along her zippered pillowcase that can easily be packed in any size suitcase. Once we arrive at our destination, I simply stuff her case full of hotel pillows or comforters. Dirty laundry can work in a real pinch, but there's no need to resort to stuffing your pillow with laundry when visiting our house; we have a plethora of pillows. We do need to warn you however, that when we pick you up from the airport in our "purple car," it's really just a gold Dodge Dart that was desperately in need of a snazzy name.

the wobbles

Dad has the wobbles. He's been to Mayo Clinic, Cleveland Clinic, and every balance disorder place around, but no one knows what's behind his problem. Like others with unknown diseases, Dad feels he should get to name this thing. He has dubbed it "the wobbles" and has declared his cure to be Heggy's chocolates (made in our hometown).

Since no real treatment is available, and pharmacy walkers and canes don't give Dad the stability he's looking for, he makes his own balance devices. It begins in the hardware store with the purchase of several broom handles and rubber crutch tips. After cutting off the threaded end of the broom handle, Dad applies a crutch tip. Most people would be satisfied with a sturdy staff at this point, but Dad has just begun. He has twenty or so staffs decorated to be "inappropriate for any occasion." Each is designed for a particular season, holiday, music or sports event. Like many executives, he never goes anywhere without his "entire staff."

For Christmas it's jingle bells glued with garland and what he calls mistletoe. To usher in spring training, Dad drilled and super glued to the top of another broom stick—not just any baseball, but a one-of-a-kind ball with Babe Ruth's autograph signed, "Babe Rooth." Not many of those around…Then there's Easter to celebrate! Dad found a loosely woven basket-type ball to go atop another stick into which he painstakingly threaded plastic Easter grass and stuffed miniature jelly beans.

Dressed in a fringed leather jacket, coyote cap, and carrying a fur-wrapped walking stick, Dad is a popular guest at the elementary schools. He gives programs about trees on Arbor Day and tells thrilling stories like the *Wolf Hunt*. So far, he's avoided being splattered with paint by P.E.T.A.

My favorite walking stick is a marketing tool Dad uses to advertise people's businesses; on it sits a hand-painted sign saying, "This Space for Rent." If you give him a dollar, Dad will thumb-tack your business card to his staff. This is a pretty good deal because, although disabled, Dad gets around a lot and seems to attract a good amount of attention. A teenaged magician re-upped for another month, saying, "George, I've gotten five gigs from your stick!"

My mom and dad are groupies for their alma mater, Mount Union College, and support every team with equal fervor. They make root beer floats to welcome the marching band back to school, and they support not only the championship football team, but are devoted fans of the less famous girls' basketball team as well. One day when I called them, Dad said, "We're just ready to walk out the door. Your mother has us going tonight to a tuba solo of all things." I thought Dad needed a walking stick that showed their support of the music program, so I bought him a broken clarinet. Starting with his base ingredients, broom handle and crutch tip, he painted it all black, added the clarinet's bell at the bottom, and fixed all the silver note-keys from the clarinet firmly to the stick. In place of a reed in the mouthpiece, he used a one-note noisemaker from a New Year's Eve toy. Dad calls this staff his bass clarinet and lets the music majors try to tune it for him.

If you're media shy, be careful in Alliance. "Interviews by George" is the name of Dad's radio show at the college, and he just might corner you into a recording booth. He found an old microphone and attached it to one of his staffs—stapling the cord in ringlets around the stick. When Dad is out and about, he pretends to interview people with his fake microphone trying to get them to comment on the quality of the vegetables at the grocery store or asking them if they'd like to sing a few bars of their favorite song.

I hope no one else ever turns up with "the wobbles." But if you're in need of a medication that won't cure you, but will take the edge off, I recommend going to Heggy's for a bag of chocolates, and with a little creativity, some glue and a hardware store, you'll be on your way. There's more than one way to have balance in your life.

conversation ping-pong

My sister Jennifer laughs when I tell her I'm shy. "You have never been shy," she says. I guess I don't pass her litmus test, because I talk to people in elevators. I defend myself, saying that people in elevators are easy; it's those adult cheerleaders and PTA moms that scare me now.

Conversation is a game to me. Ever since Jen and I were little, I've been practicing conversation by doing it for both of us. I was the one to order pizza and record the "I'm not here" message for Jen's answering machine. Over the years I've had a lot of practice talking. Now we live six hundred miles apart, yet here we stand with our telephone headsets on, as though hip to hip at the kitchen sink, musing over the nothings of life.

While chatting on the phone one day, Jen made an observation about our girls' extraverted and introverted personalities. She said, "Isn't it funny? You're raising me, and I'm stuck raising you!" Stuck! Did you notice how she considers raising extraverts as being stuck?

Although my daughter Emily is a bit quieter than her mother,

I want to encourage her in the art of conversation. It's a learned rhythm like jumping rope, waiting for that right moment to pop in as the rope slaps the pavement. Some don't take turns; others get stuck in the whir overhead and can't get out. Both a graceful entrance and exit can be hard to find, but like any sport, with practice it improves.

Emily and I get our dialog exercise in an interesting way; we play *Conversation Ping-pong* or its sister sport, *Ping-pong Poetry.* They're easy; you can play them in the car or while gardening or cleaning the house. I'd say you don't even break a sweat, but that's not exactly true—especially with the poetry. (It can get pretty tense when you're looking for a rhyme). The rules are simple. The server tosses a line of nonsense conversation to the opposing player. The receiver must think quickly on her feet, creatively answering the serve and volleying back another question to her opponent.

Emily has become an advanced player and a worthy adversary. We often pretend to be characters other than ourselves to make the game more interesting. Once while sparring in the car I asked her if she enjoyed her vacation in the Hamptons with her husband and twins. She replied, "Oh, we ended up not going to the Hamptons'. They weren't home, so we went to the Johnsons' instead."

Anything can prompt a game—even something as simple as noticing a spot on a shirt while folding laundry.

My serve... "Do you see this spot here? How do you suppose it got there?"

Emily's return…"It's not my fault; it's a disease. Have you ever heard of it? It's called Spotulism."

"Spotlulism, you say…Isn't that a genetic problem? Are there other spotaholics in your family?"

"Oh, yes, my cousin, Meg, has the worst case of Spotulism I've seen. Every one of her shirts has a necklace of stains around the collar where she wipes her face after meals."

"I believe I've seen a spot or two on her father's shirts as well."

"Yes. He tries to hide behind his wide ties and dark shirts, but I can spot a spotaholic."

"He should try that special diet where they don't eat or drink foods with color."

"I've heard of that diet! What's it called? Oh, yeah, the Spotkins diet."

The rope clicks. We grow tired of jumping. Emily finds the way out…

"Mom—that reminds me. Let's have blueberries for supper."

dying a thousand deaths

Like Elizabeth Taylor in her role as Cleopatra succumbing to the deadly kiss of the snake's venom, or Deborah Winger's tearful goodbye to her children in *Terms of Endearment*, I too have died a thousand dramatic deaths. Mine however, are dramas of my own making—played out in the "Anything's Possible Theater" of my mind.

Sometimes, when I'm feeling unappreciated by my family and friends, I create an "I'll show them death scene" where I watch my funeral from an angel's perch—listening in as the mourners admire my long life of sacrifice. I hear them sobbing regrets, wishing they'd spent more time with me and appreciated me more. In these scenarios, I always die tragically—like the time I jumped over the counter during a bank robbery to take a bullet for a teller who was a single mom. The martyred deaths always make the friends cry harder.

Change of scene now—driving alone on a long car trip. As boredom descends, I begin to wonder... I picture myself dying a slow death of uremic poisoning—the whites of my eyes turning yellow with backed up urine while I wait for an exit ramp with a decent restroom. Or I let myself imagine what would happen if I grazed the side of the car against a guard rail. Would I go into an immediate spin? What if I took off through the tall grass at sixty-five miles an hour? Would it leave those torn wakes of sod you see cutting from one side of the median to the other? Would the car go into a tumble? Perhaps a canned good would fly from the back and take me out. "Ann Baumgardner Tragically Killed by a Can of Cream of Mushroom Soup."

When I was little and home from school with a fever waiting that "eternal minute" with the thermometer in my mouth, I imagined what might happen if I disobeyed the warnings of my mother and bit into that slender glass rod. Shards of glass tearing at my lip and tickling the pink underbelly of my tongue, I imagined the mercury pooling in that little well, one droplet joining the others, forming one glorious toxic puddle.

All these death scenes—yet I don't want to die—I just want to experience completely safe, harrowing adventures and be admired to the extreme. Who wouldn't? But practicing peril makes me curious about how I'd respond in an actual emergency. Would I play the role of protector? A few years ago, when taking a walk on a country road with my sister, we came across a ferocious dog. Although in my day dreams I've jumped in front of motor vehicles to save the life of a toddler, I've never actually worked through what I'd do in this particular situation—a fierce dog, my sister, and me. Here we were, in "real life" facing a "real problem"…With lightning speed I grabbed Jen by the shoulders and moved her into position. Unfortunately for her, the secure position I held her in was directly in front of me. With each snarling approach of the dog, I repositioned her—front and center. Once clear of the bare-toothed beast, I was mortified by my behavior. All that practice I've had mentally taking bullets, leaping over bank counters, and stopping speeding cars with my knee caps didn't translate into a heroic response in a real world crisis with a canine.

To remedy this, I now rehearse the scene so if it ever happens again, I'll be ready…Taking a walk with my sister down a country lane…a fierce dog approaches…with the love that allows mothers to lift cars off their children, I hoist my sister high over my head, protecting her from the lunging chops of the rabid dog as it lunches on my fleshy calves. Just think of all the nice things my friends will say about me at my funeral after I die a horrible, foaming-at-the-mouth death of rabies. "That Ann. She was always so brave. Never one to think of herself. What will we ever do without her?"

foreword
(or backward)

I miss the Monty Python boys; pure silliness has lost its mascot. Playfulness is what I search for in life, and as my Grandpa used to say, "You'll always find what you're looking for." After all, fun is an attitude—not an activity. It's a decision.

This book reveals humorous moments in my life and in those close to me. I thought it would be more fun if you were able to join in, so I included questions in the Table of Contents that may spark memories and stories of your own.

My hope is that you have a playful spirit and won't mind looking a bit ridiculous, because from here on out the text is inverted. To the outside world, you'll look like you're reading a book upside down. When self publishing, you're free to make these kinds of decisions or mistakes—depending on your point of view. Now that we'll all look a bit absurd, I feel much better. Thank you.

If you want to read this book from the beginning,
flip the book over to the back cover and start with
the Table of Contents.

Ann Weimer Baumgardner
pretend you're normal

(but only when absolutely necessary)

LaVergne, TN USA
16 August 2009
154905LV00003B/8/P